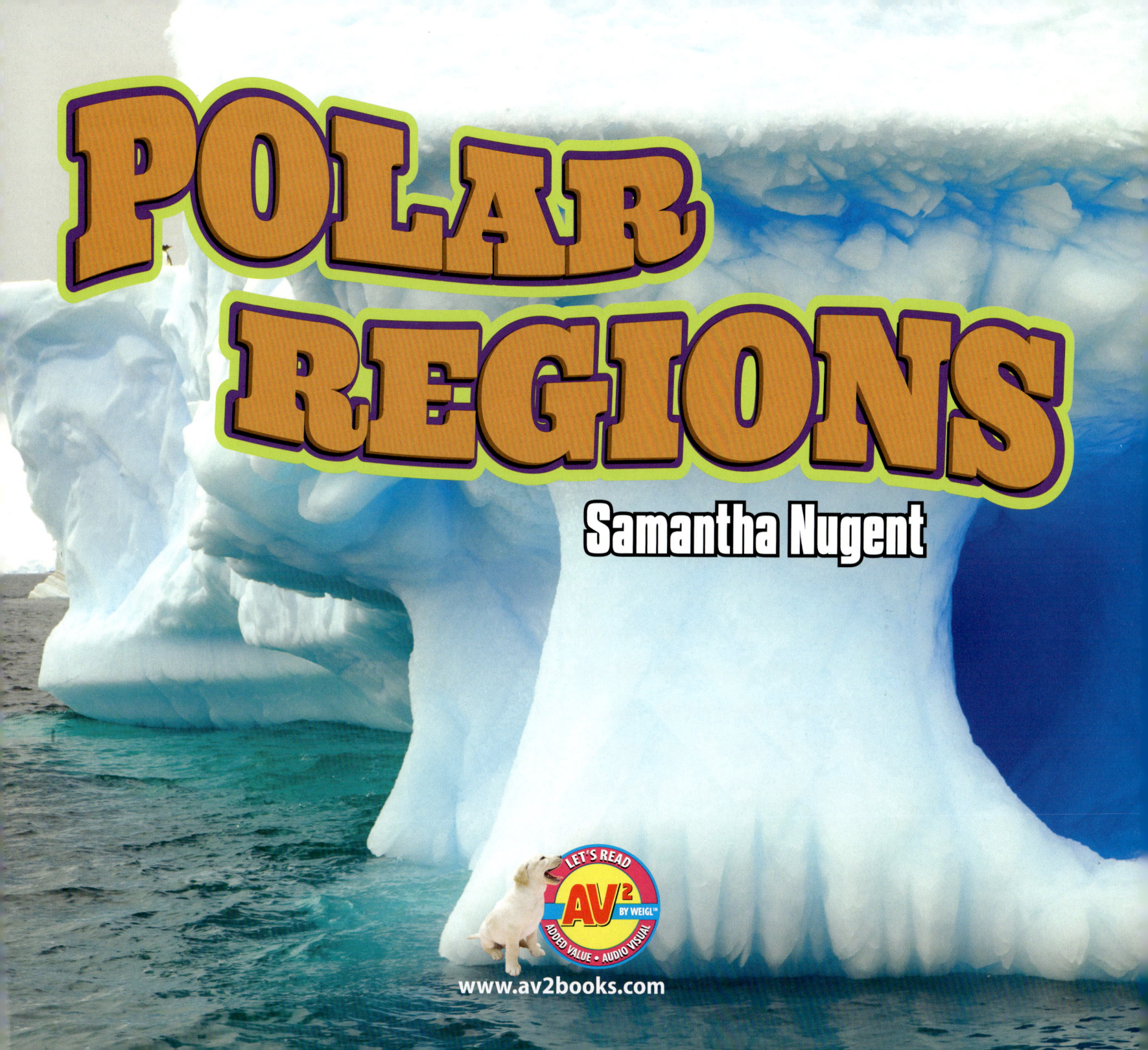

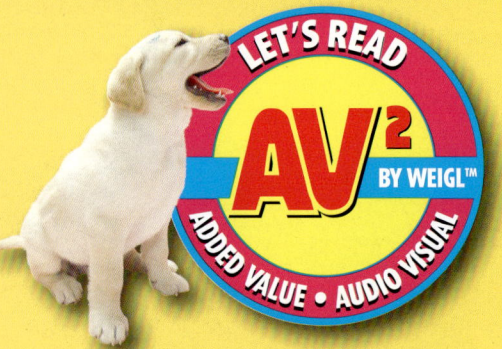

Go to www.av2books.com, and enter this book's unique code.

BOOK CODE

M288652

AV² by Weigl brings you media enhanced books that support active learning.

AV² provides enriched content that supplements and complements this book. Weigl's AV² books strive to create inspired learning and engage young minds in a total learning experience.

Your AV² Media Enhanced books come alive with...

 **Audio**
Listen to sections of the book read aloud.

 **Video**
Watch informative video clips.

 **Embedded Weblinks**
Gain additional information for research.

 **Try This!**
Complete activities and hands-on experiments.

 **Key Words**
Study vocabulary, and complete a matching word activity.

 **Quizzes**
Test your knowledge.

 **Slide Show**
View images and captions, and prepare a presentation.

... and much, much more!

Published by AV² by Weigl
350 5th Avenue, 59th Floor New York, NY 10118
Website: www.av2books.com

Copyright ©2017 AV² by Weigl
All rights reserved. No part of this publication may be reproduced, stored in a retrieval system, or transmitted in any form or by any means, electronic, mechanical, photocopying, recording, or otherwise, without the prior written permission of the publisher.

Library of Congress Control Number: 2015956117

ISBN 978-1-4896-4173-1 (hardcover)
ISBN 978-1-4896-4174-8 (softcover)
ISBN 978-1-4896-4175-5 (single-user eBook)
ISBN 978-1-4896-4176-2 (multi-user eBook)

Printed in the United States of America in Brainerd, Minnesota
1 2 3 4 5 6 7 8 9 0 19 18 17 16 15

112015   Project Coordinator: Jared Siemens
111315   Designer: Mandy Christiansen

The publisher acknowledges Corbis Images, Minden Pictures, Alamy, Getty Images, Shutterstock, and iStock as the primary image suppliers for this title.

POLAR REGIONS

Contents

- 2 AV² Book Code
- 4 What Is a Polar Region?
- 6 Where Are Polar Regions?
- 8 Polar Region Features
- 10 Polar Region Ecosystem
- 12 Plant Life
- 14 Animal Life
- 16 Auroras
- 18 Human Activity
- 20 Keeping Polar Regions Safe
- 22 Polar Region Quiz
- 24 Key Words/Log on to www.av2books.com

This is a polar region.
Polar regions are covered in snow and ice most of the year.

Polar regions are found near the North and South Poles. They are almost always very cold.

Earth's coldest temperature of −136 degrees Fahrenheit (−93 degrees Celsius) was recorded in Antarctica.

Polar regions are filled with snow and ice. Some of this snow gets pressed into giant sheets of ice.

Trees can not grow in polar regions.

Bearded seals eat clams and shrimp.

Narwhals feed on squid and fish.

A polar region ecosystem is a place made up of animals and plants that need each other in order to live.

Kelp is food for many different polar region animals.

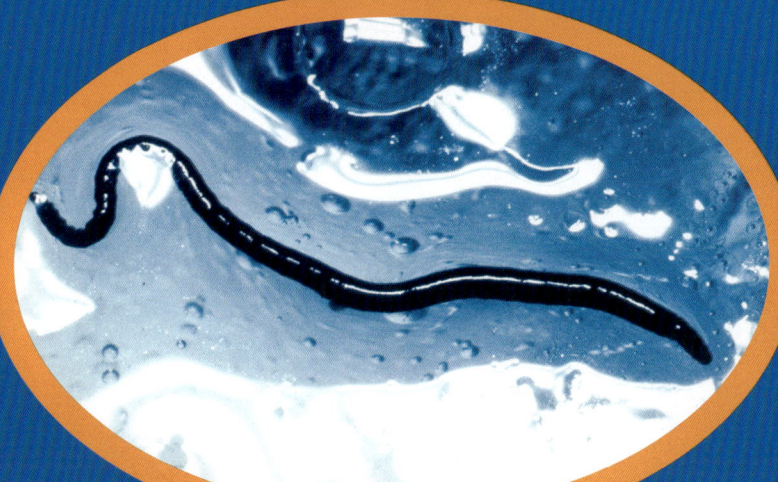

Ice worms eat algae that grow on ice.

Penguins eat krill found in ocean water.

Plants, lichens, and algae can be found in polar regions. They are an important part of a polar region ecosystem.

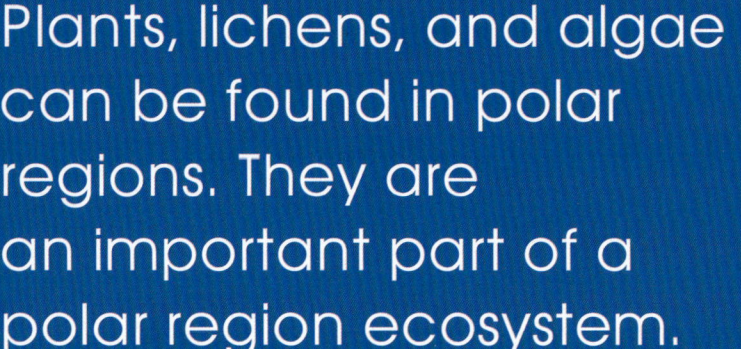

Some lichens can live more than 5,000 years.

Antarctic birds line their nests with hair grass.

Snow algae grows on snow and ice.

Arctic poppies grow in groups to stay warm.

Snow buttercups can bloom under 1 foot (30 centimeters) of snow.

13

Many different animals make their homes in polar regions.

Emperor penguins swim deeper than any other kind of bird.

Krill can live more than 200 days without food.

Sometimes the sky above polar regions glows with colorful lights. These lights are called auroras.

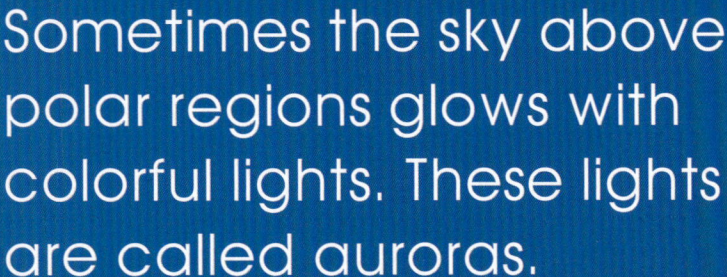

Auroras happen when gases from the Sun pass over Earth.

Fishers catch fish from polar regions for people to eat. They sometimes take too many fish from the ocean.

Whales can go hungry when fishers take too many fish from the ocean.

People move oil and goods through polar regions with ships. Animals are in danger when ships move through ocean water.

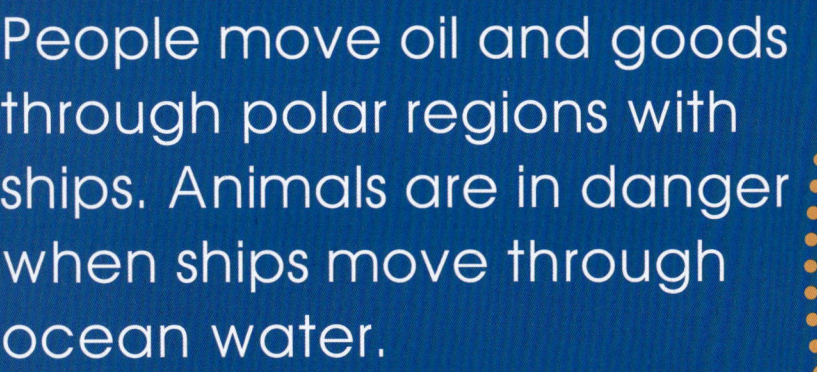

People make laws about where ships can go. These laws help keep animals safe.

Polar Region Quiz

See what you have learned about polar region ecosystems.

Find these polar region animals and plants in the book. What are their names?

KEY WORDS

Research has shown that as much as 65 percent of all written material published in English is made up of 300 words. These 300 words cannot be taught using pictures or learned by sounding them out. They must be recognized by sight. This book contains 81 common sight words to help young readers improve their reading fluency and comprehension. This book also teaches young readers several important content words, such as proper nouns. These words are paired with pictures to aid in learning and improve understanding.

Page	Sight Words First Appearance
4	a, and, are, in, is, most, of, the, this, year
7	almost, always, Earth, found, near, they, very, was
8	can, gets, grow, into, not, some, trees, with
10	eat, on
11	animals, different, each, food, for, live, made, many, need, other, place, plants, that, to, up, water
12	an, be, important, line, more, part, than, their
13	groups, under
14	any, change, has, land
15	days, homes, kind, make, without
16	above, from, lights, over, sometimes, these, when
19	go, people, take, too
20	about, goods, help, keep, move, through, where

Page	Content Words First Appearance
4	ice, polar region, snow
7	Antarctica, North Pole, South Pole, temperature
8	sheets
10	clams, fish, narwhals, seals, shrimp, squid
11	algae, ecosystem, kelp, krill, penguins, worms
12	birds, grass, lichens, nests
13	buttercups, poppies
14	albatross, bears, color, skin, wings
16	auroras, gases, sky, Sun
19	fishers, ocean, whales
20	laws, oil, ships

Check out www.av2books.com for activities, videos, audio clips, and more!

1. Go to www.av2books.com.
2. Enter book code. M288652
3. Fuel your imagination online!

www.av2books.com